Sadie's Guide To Healthy Living

© 2016 by Charlotte Fox

All Rights Reserved.

Illustrations by
Andi Kleinman, Graphic Design Artist
Flagstaff, AZ

Published by
Fox Publications, LLC
P.O. Box 22333
Flagstaff, AZ 86002

First Printing: October, 2016

Nation of Publication: United States

ISBN: 978-0-9861530-5-1

Disclaimer: The information provided within this book is for general informational and entertainment purposes only. The recipes herein are merely guidelines. The author is not a trained chef, veterinarian, or healthcare professional. She is merely a pet owner who has enjoyed looking into, and giving the very best care possible, on many levels, for her beloved Chihuahua, Sadie Elizabeth. The publisher and author are not responsible for any ill-effects, directly or indirectly as a result of the information provided herein.

No portion of this book may be reproduced for any reason, at any time, in any form, without permission from the author.

Introduction

When my children were babies, I made all of their food from organic fruits, vegetables and meats. I felt it was important to know what they were fed. They are all grown now, so my little dog, Sadie, is the recipient of my pampering.

If you aren't as concerned of what your pet eats as much as you are for yourself—you should be. Rarely does Sadie get commercially made food, but when she does, I make sure it is of the finest quality I can find. Quite often the news reports of pet food that has been recalled with a warning of how it can harm—or even cause the death of—your beloved pet. This is worrisome to me, and apparently you also, or you wouldn't be thumbing through this little book.

All the recipes in this book use the finest all-natural, organic, pesticide-free ingredients: grass-fed beef, open-range chicken, and fresh fruits and vegetables. The recipes are grain-free... and are healthy for your pet. However, if you want to use grains, there's no law against it, but choose them wisely. Not all grains are beneficial.

Don't be intimidated. It's easy to cook and bake treats for your pet—it's not rocket science, your pets won't judge you—and they will love and appreciate you for it! Plus, you'll have peace of mind knowing they're getting the very best. Have the children help you. They'll have fun making something good for their pet while learning about wholesome food.

Boné Appétit

Charlotte Fox
with expert advice from
Sadie Elizabeth

Pet Parenting

Because our pets should mean the world to us—and be a big part of it—it is important to treat them with love, kindness, patience and respect.

Pets need to know their place in their family, their responsibilities, and the parameters of their world. They need affection, companionship, exercise, a safe, healthy environment and occasionally, discipline.

In order for us to enjoy all the wonderful aspects of having pets (companionship, unconditional love, trust, etc.), pet parenting involves:

- obedience training (to keep them safe—because they can't always see the "big picture"), house training, teaching good manners around people, children, and other animals, and showing others how to be respectful around our pets.

- providing healthy food, fresh water, and a safe, clean, comfortable environment.

- insuring that our pets have plenty of playtime and exercise (and that we pick up and dispose of our pet's poop in a timely and responsible manner).

- vet visits, immunizations, and having our pets spayed or neutered.

- knowing how to use collars and leashes humanely.

- caring for sick, old or dying pets.

Pets are not disposable commodities. If you treat them well, they will be your best friends for life!

A dog is the only thing on earth that loves you more than you love yourself.

—Josh Billings

Sadie says, *"NEVER leave your pet in a hot car!"*

This Book Belongs To

_____

_____

_____

Sadie says, *"Make sure your pet feels like part of the family—they are!"*

Food Facts for Dogs

You can find extensive food lists on the Internet. This list is merely a quick-reference guide for everyday foods.

I steam, boil or bake fresh or frozen vegetables; peel, core, and remove seeds from fruit; have no sweeteners or salt in all ground nuts and seeds; I cook eggs, and de-bone cooked meats and fish.

Safe

Apples; Blueberries; Raspberries; Strawberries; Pineapples; Cantaloupe and Watermelon; Broccoli; Carrots; Celery; Cucumbers; Green Beans, Garbanzo and Kidney Beans (unsalted, canned); Red Beets; Pumpkin and Sunflower Seeds; Peanut and Hazelnut Butters; Flax Seed Meal; Chia Seeds (raw, soaked and unsalted); Leaf-flesh & Heart of Artichokes (no flowers); Asparagus; Meats and Fish; cooked Eggs; Sauerkraut; Pumpkin; Zucchini; Sweet Potatoes and Yams.

Not Safe/Toxic

Alcohol and Beer; Tree Nuts (Brazil, Hickory, Macadamia, Pecans, Pistachios and Walnuts); Avocado; Caffeine; Chives, Garlic, and Onions; Chocolate; Erythritol/Xylitol/Stevia; raw Fish; Grapes and Raisins; Mushrooms; Nutmeg; raw or green Potatoes; raw Eggs; Fruit Seeds and Pits; Rhubarb; Tomatoes; Tarragon; uncooked Yeast Dough.

Limit Or Avoid

Almond and Cashew Butter (unsalted); Dairy; Liver (this surprises me too!); Salt; Spinach; Yogurt and Cheese. (We're all guilty of masking a medicinal pill in a chunk of cheese. No worries! But remember, you could use a small piece of meat instead!)

Consult your DVM for foods that may worsen certain health conditions. And, if your pet displays signs of allergies to certain foods, avoid them.

Charlotte says, "Whole nuts, seeds and popcorn can be choking hazards. To be safe, grind or chew them first before giving to your dog. Sadie's allergic, so gets none. When snacking on popcorn, I bite off the hull part and give her the puffy part. We don't want to invite teeth problems."

Homemade Jerky

Being blessed with an amazing butcher at our Whole Foods Market, I have him trim off the fat and cut the London Broil or Chicken Breasts in nice slices that are 1/8" to 1/4" thick, so all I have to do is put it in the oven.

If you will be slicing it yourself, freeze the meat for a while (until crystallized) to make it easier to cut uniformly.

Chicken and beef are Sadie's favorites, but you can make jerky out of practically anything. Any fowl… try turkey and duck; any red meat would work… buffalo, lamb, rabbit, and if you're fortunate enough to hunt, elk, deer, mountain lion, etc. are also acceptable, as well as de-boned fish. Experiment. Find your dog's (and *your!*) favorites.

Preheat your oven to 200° F. Line a cookie sheet with tin foil or parchment paper to catch the drippings and make clean-up easier.

Place a wire rack inside the cookie sheet. This will help the air circulate better around the strips and decrease cooking time.

Lay as many of the strips on the wire rack as it will hold, making sure they don't touch.

Bake 4-6 hours, depending on how thick the slices are cut. Mine vary a tad, so as they dry and harden to desired texture, I remove them.

Blot any pools of grease that may be on the strip of meat with paper towels, then allow to cool.

Jerky strips should be completely dry and have no moisture.

Wrap the jerky in a paper towel and store in a paper bag in the refrigerator.

*Sometimes I give it a jump-start and bake at 225° F for about an hour, then lower it to the 200° F for remaining time.

Sadie says, "My bedtime snack will sometimes include a bit of crunchy organic dry dog food. I'm still young enough and have strong teeth."

Sadie's Favorite Meals

Yes, Sadie *IS* the boss of me! She and I often share the same meal. Since I eat quite simply, there is no concern about spices that may upset her system. When I do have an occasional spicy meal, Sadie has her own special leftovers. I cook what I know she likes.

Accordingly, the meal suggestions below use cooked, unseasoned, de-boned, and gristle-free meats and fish. (I never bother with shellfish and crustaceans. I'm allergic and they're iffy anyway.) I cook most vegetables—including broccoli, asparagus, yams—and artichokes are always cooked through. Sadie does like her apples and cucumbers raw (but peeled of course!) and cut in small pieces.

Chicken & Broccoli
Roast Beef & Asparagus
Salmon with Cucumbers & Carrots
Tuna or Halibut Steaks with Artichokes
Pork Roast with Yams & a tad bit of Applesauce

Some other side-dish ideas could include zucchini, garbanzo or kidney beans, beets, or a dollop of canned or fresh-cooked pumpkin.

Sprinkle a little nutritional yeast on top if you wish. Also, I add a half teaspoon of organic coconut oil on one of her daily meals, and sprinkle some enzymes, probiotics, and a supplement for plaque prevention.

On days that I juice, I will give Sadie a couple tablespoons. She loves it.

She loves strawberries, pineapples and apples, watermelon, cantaloupe, raspberries, and blueberries for dessert. ALL in moderation. About a cubic-inch worth for my Chihuahua. Always consider the size of your pet and their digestive tract.

Charlotte says, "With cooked artichokes, I scrape the meat off the leaves with either my teeth or a butter knife and feed to Sadie. She's usually on my lap during dinner, so it's easy to share with her. Do I share any of the 'heart' of the artichoke with her? Ummm... not usually—I don't want to spoil her."

Sadie's Stew

To make a stew, brown your chicken, beef or pork in a little coconut oil until mostly cooked and the pan has some of that brown deliciousness stuck on the bottom. Add enough water to cover the meat and stir. Cover and cook on low heat until desired tenderness. Then throw in some of your pet's favorite chopped vegetables. Cover and cook until done.

I include a stew, as many pets like the taste and texture of canned dog food. Once your homemade stew is cooled and ready to be eaten, you can put it all in a food processor, or mash with a fork, or however you choose to give it a 'canned-food' consistency.

Chicken Broth
Yummy! Yummy! So easy on the Tummy!

Sadie's favorite broth is made from three chicken thighs, one quart of filtered water, two stalks of celery and three or four carrots. Bring everything to a boil. Cover and cook on low heat for about four hours. Cool to room temperature.

Serve the cooled broth right away or freeze for later. Use the remaining meat and veggies like stew. After removing & discarding the chicken skin and bones, cut the meat and veggies to match your dog's size. Proportionately, you will need to add more veggies.

Raw Food Diets

Although I feel there is a place for raw-food diets, I don't follow them for meats and fish. (Some people do… we all make our own decisions.) And when it comes to vegetables, Sadie will have raw vegetables occasionally, but most of the time they are cooked (usually steamed) at least half-way through. It is easier on her digestive tract. Fruits are usually raw, but sometimes I warm them a little for her.

Sadie says, "Always have fresh water readily available for your pet."

Sadie's Gizzard Treats
(or Cooked Ground Meat of Your Choice)

Sadie loves gizzards—especially when they are fresh-cooked and ground up real fine in a meat grinder or food processor.

Basic Gizzard Treats Stage One

Bring **1 1/2 pounds of gizzards** in (2) two cups of water to a boil. Cover and simmer on low until tender (approximately one hour). Cool. Cut off majority of gristle and throw it away. Run the gizzards through a grinder (twice) to make them real fine.

If using ground meat—Brown first. Add two (2) cups of water. Cover and simmer for about an hour to make a nice broth. Cool.

Use two (2) cups firmly packed gizzards or ground meat. Mix in:

1¼ cups of the Broth from cooking the gizzards or ground meat
1 Tablespoon Nutritional Yeast
⅓ cup Golden Flaxseed Meal, ground
½ cup melted Coconut Oil
2 raw Eggs*, scrambled
⅔ cup Coconut Flour

Let sit 15 minutes. Stir.

Preheat oven to 350° F. Bake on well-greased cookie sheets.

Grease hands and roll small chunks of the dough to form balls approximately 1" in diameter. Flatten into discs about ¼" thick and place on a cookie sheet. Bake approximately 25 minutes, or until edges are a bit browned. Flip biscuits and lower the temperature to 225°. Bake another 25 minutes.

Biscuits may still seem a little soft, so crack your oven door just a tad, and continue baking so more moisture escapes and biscuits become harder and feel dry to the touch. This may take another 30 minutes.

Hint: Use all the dough for **Basic Gizzard Treats** or **divide into thirds** to make treats with fruit & veggie *Add-Ins* and/or *Chia Seed Treats*. I make all three recipes to accommodate Sadie's sophisticated palate.

Basic Gizzard Treat Add-Ins
Stage Two

Add the following *to the remaining two-thirds of the dough, then cut in half if you also want to make the Chia Seed Recipe below.*

1 cup raw Yam, finely shredded
½ cup raw Zucchini, finely shredded
½ Apple, shredded

If you want a stiffer dough, add a couple tablespoons of Garbanzo Bean Flour to desired consistency. Follow previous baking directions.

Chia Seed Gizzard Treats
Stage Three

When you add the following to the *recipe above,* this will make the firmest dough, and the hardest biscuits.

1 cup Garbanzo Bean Flour
⅛ cup Olive or melted Coconut Oil
¼ cup Chia Seeds

Place in a covered bowl in your refrigerator overnight to allow the chia seeds to soften.

The next day, add *1 Egg* (or egg replacement of your choice), to this *mixture.*

Follow the baking instructions for the *Basic Gizzard Treats* recipe.

Depending on the size you make the biscuits, the entire *Basic Gizzard Treats* recipe—including *Variations* and *Chia Seed Treats*—will make approximately four cookie sheets of biscuits.

Store all biscuits in a paper bag in your refrigerator.

*If your pet is allergic to eggs, omit eggs and add an egg-replacement product of your liking.

Helpful Hint: If you do not use all the broth from cooking the meat, freeze it for times when your dog has tummy upsets and cook rice in it.

Rise and Shine
Wakey! Wakey! I Smell Bakey!

Another favorite treat is bacon. She loves bacon—plain, or in a treat! She doesn't get this often (neither do I), as it's considered a 'processed' food, but we do indulge periodically.

Process individually in a food processor until very fine:

1/2 pound of lean Bacon, (trim fat off), fried real crisp and cooled
1/3 cup raw Asparagus (about 3 sprigs)
1/2 cup raw Zucchini

Put all in large bowl and add:

1 Tablespoon Nutritional Yeast
2 raw Eggs (or egg replacements)
1 Tablespoon Chia Seeds
1/2 cup Coconut Flour
1/4 cup Coconut Oil, melted and cooled a little

Cover and let sit 30 minutes. Form into a ball.

Preheat oven 325° F. Bake on a well-greased cookie sheet.

Tear off small chunks from ball of dough, and form into thin discs approximately 2" in diameter until all the dough is used.

Bake for about 20 minutes, then flip to brown on the other side.

Bake about another 15 minutes (or less if browned).

Crack the oven door and lower the temperature to 200° F. Bake until cooked through and dry to the touch—about another 20 minutes.

Store in a paper bag in the refrigerator.

Sadie says, "*YUM-MY!!! These treats are the BEST! They're very easy to chew... not too hard, not too soft. They're just right! I could eat a hundred of them!*"

Your Pet's Favorite Foods

Use this space to list your pet's favorite foods & snacks. You can include or substitute some of these when making your stew or treats.

_____

_____

_____

_____

_____

_____

_____

_____

_____

_____

_____

_____

_____

_____

Sadie says, *"Always be present when you're feeding your pet to be there to help in case of choking."*

Good-To-Know Tidbits

Ounces of Prevention

We are privileged to have at our disposal the use of the Internet. This can be your best friend when looking for information for your pet. I have favorites, you'll find yours. Use common sense.

Rawhide Chews

I have **NEVER** read anything good about these! Among other things, they are known to pose a choking hazard. I prefer to err on the side of caution and I **NEVER** give them to Sadie! See for yourself. Google *rawhide chews for dogs* and see what pops up.

Flea Collars

Many flea collars are extremely toxic and can make your pet ill. Choose wisely. All-natural herbal collars and sprays are available. There are many do-it-yourself recipes on the Internet too.

Toxic Fertilizers & Pesticides

Avoid all together! If your dog walks through a fertilized lawn or bushes, or through anything treated with a toxic pesticide, bathe him or her immediately with organic shampoo! Fertilizers and pesticides can be dangerous when inhaled, ingested or absorbed through the skin!

Alert! Be mindful of household cleaners, room deodorizers (I diffuse essential oils), and perfumes that are not organic in nature. They can harm *your* health and that of your pet. You can do an Internet search for names of harmful (and safe) household products.

Sadie says, "Use a harness instead of a collar when walking your pet. A harness puts less strain on their neck and gives you more control in case of a confrontation with other animals, people, or vehicles.

Naturopathic Medicine

Veterinarians definitely have their place in your pet's care and well-being. Fortunately, aside from your regular vet, there are holistic veterinarians who alternatively treat with naturopathic medicine when they can.

Sadie gets regular check-ups when necessary, but for the most part, I treat her naturopathically with my herbal tinctures, ointments, essential oils, and flower essences. I choose to follow advice from naturopathic professionals and this works beautifully for Sadie. **But one must exercise caution and common sense: this is powerful medicine!**

There are numerous books and websites to help guide you through this journey if this is the way you choose to care for your pet. **Use only well-reputed supplements suggested by a Naturopath or your DVM.** Exercise caution and common sense.

Your Pet's Allergies & Medications

_____

_____

_____

Your Pet's Supplements

Research the Internet for supplements to include in your pet's diet (gut bacteria and enzymes, in particular). Consult your Vet. I have my favorite go-to sites, and when you are searching for yours, use key phrases like *healthy pets* or *natural pet products* and key words of that nature.

_____

_____

Sadie says, "Never ignore your pets or take them for granted. Exercise them when you can. They're all precious."

Bathing and Grooming

It goes without saying this should be done on a regular basis with organic non-irritating shampoos. If your groomer doesn't supply this, bring in your own or bathe your pet yourself if you are able.

I bathe my little dog (remember to put cotton balls in the ears), and when done, wrap her in a warmed towel (just like we did with our babies). Putting a warmed rice-bag in their bed allows them to stay warm while drying. Cozy! Cozy! Also, check out *epsom salt uses for dogs* on the Internet. I just learned of how good it is for many things.

Have nails clipped regularly and anal glands expressed when necessary.

Teeth

My groomer is awesome. She gets Sadie's teeth sparkling white without unnecessary anesthesia. Too much can go wrong when you anesthetize your pet for routine cleaning.

However, anesthesia cannot be avoided if a dental condition dictates using it, i.e., teeth removal, gum disease, cleaning or other conditions where getting below the gum-line cannot be avoided. This should <u>only</u> be done by a well-reputed, Doctor of Veterinary Medicine.

And, about teeth: If your pet is an aggressive chewer, I heard recently that if they chew on something *harder* than their teeth, they can fracture them. So be careful with things like antlers, rocks, and the like.

Charlotte says, *"Think about how much you love being massaged. Besides a sense of security and well-being, there are many other health benefits for your pet with massage. Sadie loves them. How-to techniques can be found on the Internet."*

Oops! Accidents Happen!
Spot Removal ideas

First, pick up or blot up what you can.

The best homemade spot remover I've ever made (at the time I wrote this) is the following: Keep in mind that with access to the Internet, you may find one that you prefer. There are *many*.

1 pint warm water
1/4 cup Borax
1/4 cup Table Salt (I use a fine sea salt)
1/4 cup white distilled vinegar
Stir together until dissolved.

Do a test spot first, just in case!

Liberally apply to stain with a wet sponge. Scrub with a soft brush or cloth. Blot.

Let sit 20 minutes or so. Blot again.

I throw a towel over it while it dries.

Repeat if necessary.

As far as store or Internet purchases go, I've had the best luck with those that offer enzymatic cleaning and/or those that use oxidizers. An Internet search will provide you many choices. It's important to clean up as soon as possible when your pet pees.

Sadie says, *"Remember to bring poop bags with you when walking or going places with your pet. Dispose of their waste in an appropriate container. The environment (and your neighbors) will thank you for it!"*

In Case of Emergency

Copy this page on bright neon-colored paper and have one for your front door, and one for your wallet and/or inside the glove compartment of your vehicle(s).

Please Rescue My Pet(s)

My Pet(s) May Be Home Alone

Address
Phone

Name(s)	Type of Pet(s)	Description

Contact(s)

Name
Phone

Veterinarian

Address
Phone

Extra Notes to Crew
Important info about my pet(s) coloring, age, biter, illnesses, etc.

Author grants permission to copy for personal use.

Owner

Name

Address

Phone Number(s)

Pet Sitter/Caretaker

Name

Address

Phone Number(s)

In case of emergency, the above caretaker has my permission to act on my behalf for the care of my pet.

Date   Signature

_____   _____

Author grants permission to copy for personal use.

Immunization Record

For _____

Date	Immunization	Tag #

Microchip Information _____
_____

Sadie says, *"Keep shots current, & license and microchip your pet!"*
Author grants permission to copy for personal use.

YOUR PET'S PHOTO HERE

Your Pet's Name

Information

DOB	Gender Neutered / Spayed	Breed

Color & Markings

Veterinarian
Address
Phone

Emergency Contact(s)
Name(s)
Phone(s)

Pet Insurance
Company Name
Policy #
Phone

Food & Supplement Scheduling

Prescription Meds Scheduling

Special Instructions

Author grants permission to copy for personal use.

Great Gift Idea

Do you know others who would like this book?

Sadie's Guide To Healthy Living
Recipes for Happy Dogs

may be purchased from the merchant you bought this book from... or you can write to Sadie and Charlotte at the address given in the front of this book... or email the author from her website:

www.therewasone.com

Here's a little card you may duplicate
to include when you give gift copies of

Sadie's Guide To Healthy Living
Recipes for Happy Dogs

Sadie says, "Spread the word. Friends will enjoy this book, too!"

Before It's Time To Say Goodbye...

As hurtful as it is, this is a reality we may have to face one day. It will break your heart. Making arrangements for a beloved pet can be very traumatic at the time of death. It's hard when you're in the moment to deal with paperwork and all the decisions that must be made. Doing so ahead of time will free you of that part of this painful process. Ask your veterinarian for direction, or visit…

www.therewasone.com
for information on how to order

and then there was one
an in-depth workbook guide
for end-of-life planning
for both you and your pets.

Don't miss these delightful children's titles from Fox Publications, LLC available on Amazon.com

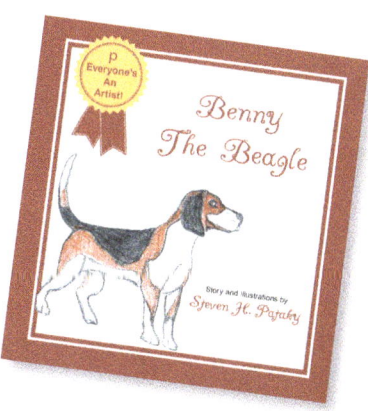

www.ingramcontent.com/pod-product-compliance
Lightning Source LLC
Chambersburg PA
CBHW040209020526
44112CB00039B/2853